GIANTS IN JEANS

Abhijit Naskar is the twenty-first century Neuroscientist whose contributions in Cognitive and Behavioral Neuroscience have helped the world tackle the issues of systemic racism, prejudice, hate, extremism, discrimination and biases more effectively. As an untiring advocate of mental health and universal acceptance, he became a beloved best-selling author all over the world with his very first book "The Art of Neuroscience in Everything". With his pioneering ventures into the Neuropsychology of beliefs and biases, he has hugely contributed in the eradication of religious and cultural differences in our world, for which he is popularly hailed as the humanitarian scientist, who takes the human civilization in the path of sweet general harmony.

GIANTS IN JEANS

100 Sonnets
of United Earth

ABHIJIT
NASKAR

Also by Abhijit Naskar

The Art of Neuroscience in Everything
Your Own Neuron: A Tour of Your Psychic Brain
The God Parasite: Revelation of Neuroscience
The Spirituality Engine
Love Sutra: The Neuroscientific Manual of Love
Homo: A Brief History of Consciousness
Neurosutra: The Abhijit Naskar Collection
Autobiography of God: Biopsy of A Cognitive Reality
Biopsy of Religions: Neuroanalysis towards Universal
Tolerance
Prescription: Treating India's Soul
What is Mind?
In Search of Divinity: Journey to The Kingdom of Conscience
Love, God & Neurons: Memoir of a scientist who found
himself by getting lost
The Islamophobic Civilization: Voyage of Acceptance
Neurons of Jesus: Mind of A Teacher, Spouse & Thinker
Neurons, Oxygen & Nanak
The Education Decree
Principia Humanitas
The Krishna Cancer
Rowdy Buddha: The First Sapiens
We Are All Black: A Treatise on Racism
The Bengal Tigress: A Treatise on Gender Equality
Either Civilized or Phobic: A Treatise on Homosexuality
Wise Mating: A Treatise on Monogamy
Illusion of Religion: A Treatise on Religious
Fundamentalism
The Film Testament
Human Making is Our Mission: A Treatise on Parenting
I Am The Thread: My Mission
7 Billion Gods: Humans Above All
Lord is My Sheep: Gospel of Human
Morality Absolute
A Push in Perception
Let The Poor Be Your God
Conscience over Nonsense
Saint of The Sapiens
Time to Save Medicine
Fabric of Humanity
Build Bridges not Walls: In the name of Americana
The Constitution of The United Peoples of Earth

Lives to Serve Before I Sleep
When Humans Unite: Making A World Without Borders
All For Acceptance
Monk Meets World
Mission Reality
Citizens of Peace: Beyond The Savagery of Sovereignty
Operation Justice: To Make A Society That Needs No Law
See No Gender
The Gospel of Technology
Every Generation Needs Caretakers: The Gospel of
Patriotism
Aşkanjali: The Sufi Sermon
Mad About Humans: World Maker's Almanac
Revolution Indomable
When Call The People: My World My Responsibility
No Foreigner Only Family
Hurricane Humans: Give me accountability, I'll give you
peace
Ain't Enough to Look Human
Servitude is Sanctitude
Time To End Democracy: The Meritocratic Manifesto
I Vicdansaadet Speaking: No Rest Till The World is Lifted
Boldly Comes Justice: Sentient not Silent
Good Scientist: When Science and Service Combine
Sleepless for Society
Neden Türk: The Gospel of Secularism
Martyr Meets World: To Solve The Hard Problem of
Inhumanity
The Shape of A Human: Our America Their America
When Veins Ignite: Either Integration or Degradation
Heart Force One: Need No Gun to Defend Society
Solo Standing on Guard: Life Before Law
Generation Corazon: Nationalism is Terrorism
Mucize Insan: When The World is Family
Hometown Human: To Live For Soil and Society
Girl Over God: The Novel
Gente Mente Adelante: Prejudice Conquered is World
Conquered
Earthquakin' Egalitarian: I Die Everyday So Your Children
Can Live

DEDICATION

To those who live a life of accountability

CONTENTS

1. Will You Be My Poetry
(Sonnet 1)

Sonnet 1

Will You Be My Poetry
(The Sonnet)

You keep calling me a poet,
I embrace the sentiment but not the title.
I may have some power over words,
But the words themselves are nothing valuable.
It's the world behind the words that matters,
A world where all walls collapse and wither.
Once you wake up to that world,
Save human, all other titles disappear.
In that world of oneness you shall discover,
My words are not the real poetry.
My true poetry is your own humanness,
I am but a reflection of your struggling humanity.
So let's get rid of this poet and reader business!
You be my poetry, I'll be your pages.

2.   Greed and World (Sonnet 2 - 4)

Sonnet 2

I Write to Destroy You
(The Sonnet)

I don't write to pamper your ego,
I don't write to give you comfort.
I don't write to teach you self-love,
I write to destroy all selfish thought.
I don't write to inspire your pride,
I don't write to cater to your insecurity.
I don't write to entertain shallowness,
I only write to abolish self-centricity.
I don't write to tickle the instaslaves,
I don't write to peddle false perfection.
I don't write to lick the privileged boots,
I write to make soldiers of self-annihilation.
My science and my art were born on the street.
That's where I learnt, all suffering is born of greed.

Sonnet 3

Greed fosters desire,
Desire further facilitates greed.
The more you entertain it all,
The more you're stuck in a suffering-spree.
Now the question to ask is,
How do we break free from this living hell?
It is rather simple and straight forward,
Refute submission to all primitive spell.
Wildlife demands selfishness,
For it's the law of primitive existence.
But the law of civilization is,
Civilized life is defined by kindness.
Stand up as human against the animal's desire.
Be the bold-spirited, unselfish world-maker.

Sonnet 4

How to build a world,
When there is no instruction manual!
You don't need no instruction,
For you are the world and the manual.
You are the creator as well as the creation,
Your two hands are hands of destiny.
Once you set your mind to building a society,
All peddlers of division will beg for mercy.
You are not the second coming,
For you are the first and one of a kind.
Holding the hands of these firsts through ages,
The world advances leaving savageries behind.
This my friend is the motto of world-building,
Live life as a future human amidst bigoted vermin.

3. Errors and Correction
(Sonnet 5 - 7)

Sonnet 5

Sonnet of Enlightenment

World is born when individual is born.
Individual is born when collectivity is realized.
Collectivity is realized when selfishness is erased.
Selfishness is erased when love is universalized.
Love is universalized when separation is destroyed.
Separation is destroyed when superstition is crushed.
Superstition is crushed when reason is nourished.
Reason is nourished when correction is desired.
Correction is desired when ignorance is recognized.
Ignorance is recognized when arrogance is abolished.
Arrogance is abolished when humility is fostered.
Humility is fostered when simplicity is habit.
Simplicity is habit when awareness awakens.
Awareness awakens when expansion awakens.

Sonnet 6

Expansion is health,
Expansion is sanity.
Contraction is sickness,
Contraction is animality.
In expansion there is civilization,
In expansion there is humanity.
Defy everything that makes you narrow,
Defy everything that facilitates bigotry.
Expansion is another name for life,
The life of a human who's responsible.
Animals can practice errors as tradition,
But for a human self-correction is highest struggle.
Self-correction wipes out all walls of division.
Lesser the walls greater the expansion.

Sonnet 7

Sonnet of Moronity

Eraser is not for the one,
Who makes an error.
Eraser is for the one,
Who is a self-corrector.
Hence pages of our paradigm are filled,
With many heinous mistakes.
While some of them are born of implicit bias,
Most are just plain boneheadedness.
It is one thing to be stoked about progress,
And quite another to be aware of its purpose.
If we forget the point behind it all,
Vultures will feed on our fancy carcass.
Purpose of progress is to lift all humanity,
Not to pamper the elites' moronity.

4. Billion-Dollar Grave
(Sonnet 8 - 10)

18

Sonnet 8

Elitism is moronism,
For it facilitates disparity.
A world built to worship the elites,
Is a kingdom infested with moronity.
Call yourself human the day,
A billionaire and a janitor are equal to you.
Until then with every bit of your snobbery,
You are only making disparities brew.
Equity, justice and inclusion,
All begin not in the Capitol but at home.
Even alone, if you can practice those tenets,
That's when your sentience is truly honed.
To a struggling stranger if you cannot lend a hand,
Our world will remain a decadent wasteland.

Sonnet 9

Thread by thread fabric is made.
Heart by heart community is made.
Star by star the sky is made.
Shoulder to shoulder the world is made.
The power of one is the power of all,
Wilderness is another name for divisionism.
When we are together we are civilized,
Civilization is synonym for nonsectarianism.
But the tragedy of the world is,
Each thread thinks they are all important.
And the problems faced by others,
Are all considered insignificant.
A world where callousness is assumed cool,
Is but a billion-dollar grave of the fool.

Sonnet 10

Billion-Dollar Grave

(The Sonnet)

All our life we work hard to buy golden chains.
With which we then bind ourselves.
What's the point of living as fancy slaves?
What will we do with our billion-dollar graves?
We sit on our couch covering our eyes,
Then we yell, why everything is so very dark!
But no one hears for they are also shouting,
Praying for a messiah to bring back life's spark.
We've forged fascist fences out of all our gold,
And have placed them as walls around us.
Then we shout out - help, help,
And beg to be saved by the universe!
Greed of dollar is the toxic mold on the green of life.
Life flourishes on moderation, not consumerist strife.

5. Business and Consumerism
(Sonnet 11 - 13)

Sonnet 11

Sonnet of Consumerism

Ever wonder in a world of consumerism,
Who's the consumer, who's the product!
You may think that you are the one owning things,
But it's the things that own you, head and heart.
When unmoderated materialism is the world's norm,
Consumer is the product, product does the consuming.
And this insanity is revered as industrial growth,
Then they wonder, why is there so much suffering!
The point is, your insecurity is good for business,
The shallower you are, the more your pocket empties.
But if you don't wanna end up at la casa de loco,
Stop living in products and focus on memories.
Corporations chasing revenue cause economic disparity.
Buy less, buy local, to construct a sustainable economy.

Sonnet 12

If you wanna see economic equity,
Start by supporting your local business.
One small business in one small neighborhood,
Is the backbone of sustainable economic progress.
Amplifying revenue by catering to emptiness,
Is the mark of a stone-age transaction.
There is nothing wrong in producing revenue,
But it mustn't come through exploitation.
Business is good for social advancement,
But business without humanity is regress.
Most companies see consumer welfare secondary,
Their goal is to increase the number of slaves.
Corporate social responsibility is only a PR stunt.
Business with warmth lasts forever in people's heart.

Sonnet 13

Against Nothing
(The Sonnet)

I am not against consumerism,
I am not against corporations.
I am not against politics and policy,
I am not against politicians.
I am not against fame and fortune,
I am not against celebrity.
I am not against entrepreneurship,
I am not against technology.
I am not against bureaucrats,
I am not against red tape.
I am not against bibles and comics,
I am not against prayers and faith.
I ain't against anything that serves human welfare.
The moment they go astray, I'll be their nightmare.

6. Development and Universalism
(Sonnet 14 - 16)

Sonnet 14

Environment and Development
(The Sonnet)

Environment is not more important than development,
Development is not more important than environment.
Since we no longer live in the wilderness as animals,
We must make both work together in agreement.
Why do we need to wipe out forests and lakes,
To lay the foundation for growth and prosperity!
With our achievements in science and tech,
We can build modern cities nestled in greenery.
Unfortunately, once the green of dollar starts rolling in,
Green of nature goes out of the window.
The real problem is the mindset of profits over people,
It has nothing to do with our desire to grow.
Let us find harmony between concrete and nature.
Without harming earth, let us build green skyscrapers.

Sonnet 15

I am the craftsman,
I am the craft.
I am the artist,
I am the art.
I am the infinity,
I am absolution.
I am impossibility,
I am the solution.
I am the just,
As well as justice.
I am equality,
As well as its means.
There's always a way, so long as I exist,
And I exist wherever there's a Universalist.

Sonnet 16

In case you are wondering,
What is a universalist!
Let me make it very clear,
It is one who lives above all ist.
Then you may question,
Isn't universalism another ism!
To which I ask you,
Is drinking water hydrationism?
There's a ton of words,
That we are compelled to use.
But to realize life,
We must step across linguistic abuse.
Still if universalism causes in you friction,
Let us just call it assimilation.

7. Words and Humility
(Sonnet 17 - 19)

Sonnet 17

I've said this before, I'll say it again,
Don't be rigid with words and terminology.
Take the leap across language,
Then you shall witness life's vivacity.
Words serve their purpose,
When you use them to erase divide.
In every other situation,
Words and terms cause nothing but strife.
This comes from a person,
Whose very life is rooted in words.
If I can consider words secondary,
So can you break your wordly walls.
Leave the fight over words to couch philosophers.
Much work remains for us the world builders.

Sonnet 18

Sonnet of Grammar

Grammar, Oh Grammar,
Whatever you are,
Go away and bother,
The intellectual scholar.
I ain't no intellectual,
Nor am I a scholar,
So bother me not,
With your snobbish affair.
My words come from the soil,
My structure is born on the street.
I didn't even graduate college,
What do I know about literary creed!
Time has come for me to put you in place.
Be an aid to discourse, not an uptight nutcase!

Sonnet 19

Be humble to the lowly,
And gentle to weak.
Be a dinosaur to the phony,
And a stone wall to the critic.
It is a mad, mad world,
Where the naïve is up for abuse.
Be naïve and simple on the inside,
But learn when it's time to act a douche.
Some bullies only understand strength,
If needed keep your strength at hand.
A few firm roars of your conviction,
Will make the oppressors wet their pants.
But be very cautious while using your strength,
Reckless power turns even a saint into tyrant.

8.   Loving and Living (Sonnet 20 - 22)

Sonnet 20

Who's the saint, who's the tyrant,
Is not determined by the show of strength.
Real mark of human character,
Lies in your gentleness radiant.
The strongest souls on earth,
Keep their strength hidden unless needed,
Whereas the shallow and the entitled,
Walk around trotting over the hearts of the helpless.
Turning the other cheek to the oppressor,
May work in a world of fairies.
In our primitive world of organic apes,
Turning the other cheek means aiding inhumanities.
Love is the only answer, there is no question,
But it is a lover's duty to stand up to oppression.

Sonnet 21

In what world love means complacency?
Definitely not a human world.
In what world love means tolerating hate?
Definitely not a human world.
In what world love means allowing more harm?
Definitely not a human world.
In what world love means agreeing with bigots?
Definitely not a human world.
In what world love means aiding barbarians?
Definitely not a human world.
In what world love means supporting superstition?
Definitely not a human world.
Being loving doesn't mean letting the hate continue.
It means standing up to make all hate stop with you.

Sonnet 22

If the world is messed up,
We may not be the cause of it.
But if we die leaving it the same,
We are nothing but bags of wind.
Society wasn't built on equity,
Nor was it built on principles of justice.
All was founded on exploitation of the lowly,
And some modern apes still can't get over it.
Till today the rich talk about equality,
While flying in their private jets.
Things get even more hypocritical and wacky,
When they talk about climate change.
However, we can still make this world better,
We just have to actually start living simpler.

9. Simple Life and Shabby Clothes
(Sonnet 23 - 25)

Sonnet 23

Simple life starts with a simple heart,
A heart not congested with selfish desire.
The more you have things that you want,
The less you have things that matter.
Sooner or later we gotta grow up,
However chances are that we won't.
And when that is the case for humankind,
I'm terrified of what's headed our civilized coast.
Materialism has made a mockery of sanity,
Industry has flourished upon that mockery.
Such insanity may have suited our ancestors,
But does it suit pedestrians of universality!
I don't want you to weep over our failures.
All I ask, let's advance not as slaves but world builders.

Sonnet 24

Who is to build the world?
Who is to raise the society?
Who is to water the plants?
Who is to stand up for sanity?
Who is to bear agony for community?
Who is to go hungry feeding another?
Who is to heal the sick while bleeding?
Who is to lift the lowly trotting fire?
Who is to burn alive to bring light?
Who is to walk on thorns to build the bridge?
Who is to be deceived yet stay humble?
Who is to lay down so others can climb the ridge?
It is you, o misfit, o explorer of impossibility,
Even if no one joins us, our world is our responsibility!

Sonnet 25

Wanna know about people's character?
Walk around in shabby clothes.
Wanna know who's wise, who's egotistical?
Be the dumbest despite your brainforce.
Never try to impress people.
The more you try, the more they lose interest.
Nourish your warmth and kindness instead,
Those who care will reach out themselves.
But always remember one little thing,
You can either have life or calculation.
Calculate where it's needed,
But not in every situation.
Lovers and soldiers are the only ones living,
Rest of society is just dehydrating.

10. Love, Life and Charity
(Sonnet 26 - 28)

Sonnet 26

H2O may be water of earth,
But water of heart is love.
Without love the land of heart,
Ends up as infertile dirt.
So I say to you, oh being of heart,
Never be a miser in matters of love!
Give out love to family and stranger alike,
The more you give the more you'll have!
Love is the only thing in the world,
That dries up the more you try hoarding.
Be a robeless hobo if needed,
But never restrain your spree of giving.
Now let me tell you a secret of advanced economy.
Only with giving shall we wipe out financial disparity.

Sonnet 27

Sonnet of Charity

Charity doesn't end disparity,
It only postpones it.
Giving doesn't mean only giving,
It means lifting the fallen spirit.
With one hand help those in need,
With another treat their environment.
Don't just give money to the destitute,
Lift them up so they could help themselves.
The greatest charity in the world,
Is to help someone become self-reliant,
So that they do not need charity,
From anyone ever again.
Purpose of charity is not to build a world of charity,
Purpose of charity is to end the need for charity.

Sonnet 28

Kindness is saneness,
All else is vainness.
Better kind and be deceived,
Than live with emptiness.
To have a life of joy,
Be joy to others.
Your life will be truly whole,
When you stand up for another.
Life isn't a product,
That you can find at BestBuy.
You shall discover life when,
For others your pleasures go awry.
Pleasure has nothing to do with human life.
Life is in helping others and relieving their strife.

11. Earth, Mars and Progress
(Sonnet 29 - 31)

Sonnet 29

Awake, Arise and Walk the Talk,
Be the reason for someone's smile.
Read a few books, you'll live a little,
Help another and you'll live a lifetime.
Kindness is the only sign of life,
Not a lifestyle of luxury and riches.
Despite having all if you don't know to help,
You're but an animal of the wilderness.
What is the point of a life,
That has no bearing on social uplift!
Accountability is humanity,
Indifference is mark of an egotist.
Whole world is hometown for the being who's human.
But for self-obsessed savages even the hood is martian.

Sonnet 30

Earth and Mars, what is the difference,
Mars is barren, Earth isn't much behind!
Mars is barren for there's no advanced species,
Earth is made barren by its native intelligent kind.
We haven't yet learnt to take care of Earth,
Yet we are now headed for Mars as colonizer.
With the money it'll take to get to Mars,
We can literally end world hunger.
Mark you, I am not against space exploration,
But there's what I call existential priority.
I guess robots who vacation at high altitude,
Are least likely to fathom what's humanity.
Advancement that ignores human suffering,
After a brief flight, eventually brings universal ruin.

Sonnet 31

Progress is a messy term,
Which in theory means ascension.
But in practice it means serving the wealthy,
And to hell with the rest of the humans!
When reckless monkeys start making rockets,
They behave like some fancy junkie.
When nuts and bolts hypnotize the apes,
Equity, justice and honor feel secondary.
Traditions have been ruling human behavior,
Now technology has cast a spell on society.
Just like mindless traditions are dangerous,
Heartless technology is injurious to humanity.
Traditions and technology both can be a boon,
Yet as of today, they sustain a world of fools.

12. Tradition and Discord
(Sonnet 32 - 34)

Sonnet 32

Some people still say,
Women belong in the kitchen.
By that same logic,
Men belong in the jungle.
Traditions of yesterday
Cannot be the standard for today,
Ethics and logic of primitives,
Cannot be the measure of civilized way.
Each generation must find themselves,
They must rewrite their own code.
Better to die in the course of ascension,
Than to survive in hypnotized mode.
Cut off all allegiance to the dead and dark,
As new humans build your own moral arc.

Sonnet 33

For rotten corpses tradition is life,
For heartless robots greatest faculty is logic.
Yet it is combining tradition and logic,
Shall we emerge as beings sapient and heroic.
We must use reason to scrutinize tradition,
We must use warmth to moderate logic.
When we put reason and warmth together,
We are endowed with powers terrific.
Sometimes we gotta compromise logic,
Sometimes we gotta compromise tradition.
We shall recognize which is needed when,
When we live as wholesome human.
It all begins when we throw rigidity overboard,
Opposing nothing that reduces discord.

Sonnet 34

Be the breaker of discord,
Be the maker of harmony.
Be the taker of agony,
Be the giver of amity.
Be the light to the dark,
Be the might to the meek.
Be the kite to the fallen,
Be the sight for 'em to peek.
Be the heart that burns bright,
Be the hand that answers plight.
Be the feet that ignore fright,
Be the head that walks upright.
Rather than being a lazy descendant,
Be the reason for a future radiant.

13. Time and Competition
(Sonnet 35 - 37)

Sonnet 35

Future is just imagination,
And the past is nothing but memory.
But what we must keep in mind is,
The present contains the infinity.
Present is called present,
For it holds the gift of creation.
You decide whether you'll use it to create,
Or waste it on anxiety and illusion.
Draw lessons from the past,
As well as from futuristic imaginations.
But do not let them cripple you,
As illusory obstructions to action.
Feet firmly on present spread your sight far and wide,
And you shall rise as the master of time and tide.

Sonnet 36

Time and tide rule the coward,
While the valiant makes their own time.
Take it slow and be the flow,
Leave the racing to the boneless slime.
Those who say that competition is good,
Are but primitives whose religion is dollar.
A world founded on soulless competition,
Will never be free from societal disorder.
Have some regard for the worth of life,
Dishonor it not by treating as NASCAR.
Feel, think and behave as a human being,
Not as a preprogrammed teleprompter.
The rivers and birds fear no competition,
Yet without them the world cannot function.

Sonnet 37

Sonnet of Nature

What do the rivers do?
Give water for our thirst.
What do the trees do?
Give air for our lungs.
What do the animals do?
Give food for our tummy.
What do the flowers do?
Give fragrance for our body.
After taking everything,
From every member of nature,
What do we pompous idiots do?
Destroy all natural order.
It's high time to get our act together.
Nature doesn't need us, but we need her.

14. Will and Submission
(Sonnet 38 - 40)

Sonnet 38

Sonnet of Renewable Energy

There is a plug point in the sky,
Which is beaming electricity 24/7.
Yet we drill holes into the earth,
To suck oil and power our concrete heaven.
When humankind first started drilling,
They had no idea of its implication.
But eventually scientists raised warnings,
Yet drilling continued due to lack of efficient solution.
Fossil fuel has already damaged the climate,
And we no longer have time for scholarly fight.
So I say to scientists, engineers and entrepreneurs,
Come up with affordable home solar-grid.
Electric cars won't do anything for climate emergency,
Unless all electricity comes from renewable energy.

Sonnet 39

The greatest renewable energy,
Is the power of human will.
If we are truly willing for reform,
Nothing in the world can make us kneel.
But we've grown accustomed to complacency,
And indifference feels rather pleasant.
That's why we let brutality continue,
While we pretend to be absolutely innocent.
This callousness has become our curse,
It has kept us apes from evolving.
If we are to ever become actually human,
To inhumanity we must stop complying.
All humanity is born of the individual.
If we are responsible so will be the world.

Sonnet 40

It has become a habit to kneel,
You keep kneeling wherever it's convenient.
Then when your submission is exploited,
You wonder why the world is so deviant.
If you want corruption to stop,
Stop facilitating it with your submission.
Instead of being a jellyfish all your life,
Feel the backbone and stand up as human.
The term human carries a lot of weight,
But in today's world it only carries dead weight.
That's because being vegetable is rather easy,
Whereas being human requires to be sentient.
So stop bending at every little situation.
Every time you bend, you break civilization.

15. Prejudice and Animals
(Sonnet 41 - 43)

Sonnet 41

Whatever doesn't adapt gets extinct,
But this doesn't mean adapting to inhumanity.
In fact, if living requires adapting to inhumanity,
Better die revolting than live with complacency.
In every situation ask yourself,
Is compromise at the best interest of society!
And whatever your whole conscience answers,
In that particular situation act accordingly.
We may compromise facts and reason,
When we are amidst warm people of faith.
We may compromise faith and belief,
When amidst freethinkers who know no hate.
But remember that under no circumstances,
We are to bow before hate and prejudices.

Sonnet 42

Once you start listening to prejudice,
Prejudice stops listening to you.
Once you slip into the stereotypical curve,
Stereotypes start to own the whole of you.
None of us are immune to prejudice,
That includes yours truly.
Human brain concocts prejudices,
To ensure our survivability.
Prejudices are assumptions,
That constitute the whole of perception.
Very little of our mind's reality,
Is actually free from bias and superstition.
Though we can never be fully free from prejudice,
With reason we can learn to distinguish it.

Sonnet 43

When we know not we are prejudiced,
There is no question of treating it.
When we know not we are biased,
There is no question of overcoming it.
When we know not we are bigoted,
There is no question of humanizing.
When we know not we are self-obsessed,
There is no question of universalizing.
When we know not we are sectarian,
There is no question of being nonsectarian.
When we know not we are inhuman,
There is no question of being human.
Humanity begins with the awareness of animality,
First know we are animals, then act towards diversity.

16. Jungle and Collective
(Sonnet 44 - 46)

Sonnet 44

Diversity brings prosperity,
Tribalism brings tragedy.
Inclusivity brings harmony,
Exclusion brings anxiety.
Amity brings serenity,
Prejudice brings insecurity.
Affection binds community,
Mistrust breaks sanity.
Kindness kindles kinship,
Hate brews fiendship.
Goodness grows heartship,
Arrogance fosters bruteship.
Gentle beings make a gentle world.
Until it's realized, we're stuck in a jungle vault.

Sonnet 45

Who makes us primitive - nature.
Who keeps us primitive – ourselves.
Who makes us ignorant – nature.
Who keeps us ignorant – ourselves.
Who makes us tribal – nature.
Who keeps us tribal - ourselves.
Who makes us stereotypical – nature.
Who keeps us stereotypical – ourselves.
Who makes us narrow – nature.
Who keeps us narrow – ourselves.
Who makes us wild – nature.
Who keeps us wild – ourselves.
Nature still dictates plenty on how we apes move.
But she has also given us the power to improve.

Sonnet 46

Love is in everybody,
Not everybody is in love.
Power is in everybody,
Not everybody can power-up.
Everybody loves beautiful clothes,
Few care for heart's beauty.
Everybody is obsessed with liberty,
Few can bear the responsibility.
Everybody lives amidst the collective,
Only few practice collectivism.
Everybody talks about the world,
Not everybody has the world in them.
Poor is not the one whose pocket is empty,
But the one whose heart lacks comity.

17. Donkeys and Dinosaur
(Sonnet 47 - 49)

Sonnet 47

Walk up to death,
And smile at your doom.
At the sight of your conviction,
Stars will begin to bloom.
Tread bravely on misery,
Defy anything that causes weakness.
At the sound of your courageous footsteps,
The soil will regain its fragrance.
Embolden your chest o mighty victor,
Against a hailstorm of ridicule.
Even the slight sound of your whisper,
Will give chills to the cruel.
Care for society, not its opinion of you.
Sacrifice all image and status, and stand up anew.

Sonnet 48

It's not about whether good things happen to you,
But whether you're a force for good to another.
It's not about whether you go to church,
But whether you're the answer to someone's prayer.
It's not about whether you make a name for yourself,
But whether you lose your character in the process.
It's not about whether your dreams come true,
But whether you forget to live as a rat in the race.
It's not about whether you bow to authority,
But whether you compromise dignity to be accepted.
It's not about whether you move fast enough,
But whether you rise up after being defeated.
The world is full with fake mottos to sustain submission.
Be a dinosaur of destiny and destroy all snobbish notion.

Sonnet 49

Vegetables have destiny,
Humans have responsibility.
Vermin have luxury,
Humans have simplicity.
Nightcrawlers have insecurity,
Humans have dignity.
Bedbugs have stability,
Humans have community.
Donkeys have self-love,
Humans have self-annihilation.
Horses have competition,
Humans have revolution.
Fancy castles of glass belong in fairy-story.
No time to rest, we have too much duty.

18. Humanhood and Cancellation
(Sonnet 50 - 52)

Sonnet 50

The more you philosophize the fundamentals of life,
The more you lose the fundamentals of life.
The more you intellectualize the essentials of life,
The less you fathom the essentials of life.
The more you dogmatize love and kindness,
The more you destroy love and kindness.
The more you argue over virtue and goodness,
The less you actually practice virtue and goodness.
The more you fight over whose ideology is the best,
The more your ideology breeds problem not solution.
The more you boast about your own culture,
The more you move astray from cultural integration.
Humans are those who place humanity above all else.
Till you realize this, you are stuck in your tribal mess.

Sonnet 51

Comfort doesn't make you grow,
Only crisis does that.
Convenience doesn't strengthen character,
Only catastrophe does that.
A candle is safe when it's not burning,
But that is not why it exists.
A ship stays steady when it's at the dock,
But its life is in the open seas.
Diamond isn't born amidst concrete luxury,
It is born in the hardship of wilderness.
A human mind isn't truly born,
Till it conquers its luxurious reliance.
If not the world, be responsible for your neighborhood.
Someone somewhere is in need of your humanhood.

Sonnet 52

Humanhood isn't him, her or them,
Humanhood requires realization beyond sex.
Pronouns may be a step in the right direction,
But they are not passport for arrogance and disrespect.
The purpose is to erase hate from society,
And we ain't gonna do that by passing judgment.
If we want there to be equity and acceptance,
We must learn to trample first our own arrogance.
Rebelling for the sake of rebelling achieves nothing,
Arrogance only produces just another bitter creature.
In trying to fight against prejudice and oppression,
Be cautious that you don't end up as the new oppressor.
Revolution is the foundation of civilization's evolution,
But it must be rooted in gentleness, not cancellation.

19. Agony and Human Nature
(Sonnet 53 - 55)

Sonnet 53

If you call me liberal,
You have understood nothing.
If you call me conservative,
You have understood nothing.
If you call me religious,
You have understood nothing.
If you call me atheist,
You have understood nothing.
If you call me communist,
You have understood nothing.
If you call me capitalist,
You have understood nothing.
You'll never find me in your fancy ideology,
You'll know me by taking pain to wipe another's agony.

Sonnet 54

It is human nature to shed tears in agony,
But taking pain to wipe another's tear is humanity.
It's human nature to be sad at the loss of something,
But giving up all to lift another is humanity.
It is human nature to reply harm with more harm,
But to stand unbending without violence is humanity.
It is human nature to reply argument with argument,
But knowing when to lose an argument is humanity.
It is human nature to win by dragging others down,
But defying competition to live a purpose is humanity.
It is human nature to blame disparity on politicians,
But to step up ensuring equity in one's area is humanity.
Just because it's human nature, doesn't make it civilized.
We shall be civilized when we are no longer hypnotized.

Sonnet 55

Selfishness is superstition,
Unselfishness is civilization.
Luxury is savagery,
Simple living is rejuvenation.
To live one must consume,
But over-consumption is sickness.
Gratification without moderation,
Ruins all internal wellness.
Freedom is not only life's treasure,
It is also a great responsibility.
Clothes and appearance come later,
There's no human without accountability.
Focus on the mettle of the human within,
Only then we'll be more than a selfish fiend.

20. Bad Samaritan and Integrity
(Sonnet 56 - 58)

114

Sonnet 56

Where the human is accountable,
There flourishes civilization.
Where the human is selfish,
There looms degradation.
Where the human has tasted sanity,
No possession can cause distraction.
Where the human has felt the joy of sacrifice,
Annihilation becomes the only ambition.
What does a world of self-obsession know,
About drunkenness of the lover!
A world run by cold facts and blind faith,
Considers the greedy to be sober.
So I say, to hell with such self-centric soberness,
I am better off with my life of madness.

Sonnet 57

Who is mad, who is sane,
Who's gonna decide it for whom?
In a world run by judgmental fools,
Disparity is hailed as the rule.
Luxury thrives on disparity,
Greed thrives on materialism.
That's why the paradigm we live in,
Labels kindness as impractical altruism.
Better be an impractical fool with warmth,
Than a dead ribcage without a heart.
Better be a law-defying bad samaritan,
Than a complacent bag of lard.
Only sign of sanity is in mad humanity.
Stand tall o brave, as an epitome of integrity!

Sonnet 58

Integrity doesn't come from wallet,
It comes from your character.
Yet you continue to value dollar,
Putting character on the back-burner.
Then you scream at the politicians,
For all the disparities and despair.
Never for a second you consider,
To distinguish need from desire.
More you pursue dollars and products,
Better it is for the corporate fraternity.
Your desire for limitless comfort,
Ruins you and makes them super wealthy.
Dial down your pursuit of convenience,
And then you'll experience the surge of sentience.

21. Integration and Disintegration
(Sonnet 59 - 61)

Sonnet 59

Suits and boots are not sentience,
Manners and etiquettes are not culture.
Intellect and technology are not progress,
Faith and tradition are not character.
Now that we've put them out of the way,
Let's talk about the matter of significance.
If you ask what that matter is,
I am talking about internal exuberance.
What is science without human warmth,
What is faith without some reason!
What is technology without community,
What is tradition without ascension!
All these are okay in their own place,
But they must be practiced with sapience.

Sonnet 60

Just because we call ourselves sapiens,
Doesn't mean we are actually sapient.
Just because we call ourselves advanced,
Doesn't mean we are not deviant.
Having an advanced brain,
Is not the same as being advanced.
When all brain is wasted on self-centricity,
We only drift away from life's vivid path.
Life is not about mechanization,
Life is not about the pursuit of comfort.
Animal life may run on self-preservation,
Either you are human or self-absorbed.
To wipe out the self is my greatest ambition.
Birth of human is in benevolent disintegration.

Sonnet 61

Integration lies in disintegration,
Where the I ends there the US begins.
Harmony lies in annihilation,
Where the tribe ends there the globe begins.
Whatever suited our ancestors,
Is not compatible with a modern society.
You can either have allegiance to borders,
Or you can have serenity and amity.
Pledging allegiance to a rag on a pole,
Is no longer a sign of well-built character.
If you wanna slogan for anything at all,
Let us slogan for sentiments beyond border.
Though born tribals, let's aim towards universality.
Let's end all foul traditions of tribal identity.

22. Identity and Principles
(Sonnet 62 - 64)

Sonnet 62

What is my identity?
What is your identity?
Why bother with all that nonsense,
Let us focus first on humanity.
Your birthplace isn't your identity,
Your culture isn't who you are.
Who you are is defined by your action,
Your conduct defines your character.
A gentle janitor is more human,
Than a condescending scientist.
A kind waitress is more human,
Than a cold, billionaire elitist.
Clothes, culture, creed, all are expendable.
Better be dead than compromise principle.

Sonnet 63

What are we without principles,
Nothing but a bag of animal flesh.
What are we without reason,
Nothing but tradition's infectious abscess.
What are we without warmth,
Nothing but insects chasing self-centricity.
What are we without collectivity,
Nothing but mechanics of monstrosity.
What are we without humility,
Nothing but a bunch of smart nimrods.
What are we without moderation,
Nothing but poisonous arthropods.
Higher the sentience, greater the responsibility,
A mind oblivious to this, is oblivious to humanity.

Sonnet 64

Let us be oblivious to security and comfort,
In our pursuit and practice of humanity.
Let us be oblivious to personal happiness,
In our endeavors into the impossibility.
Let us throw all fear and anxiety overboard,
For the dreams that'll determine our destiny.
Let us trample every foul desire for luxury,
And treat the hard problem of inhumanity.
Let us pay no heed to gain and pain,
In our course of constructing a whole society.
Let us not sit around praying for a messiah,
And stand up ourselves to carry out that duty.
Let others be oblivious to humanity if they want.
Even if it's doomsday, sapling of service we'll plant.

23. Doomsday and Flagmania
(Sonnet 65 - 67)

Sonnet 65

Doomsday is not when the earth collapses,
Nor is it the contagion of a deadly virus.
Doomsday is when humans forget humanity,
As such all of us are doomsday descendants.
There is no such thing as fall of humanity,
For humankind never rose to civilization.
Our ancestors were savages with bow and arrow,
We are modern savages with nuclear ammunition.
Each of us are raised as an incarnate of doom,
Through our veins flow the germs of selfishness.
Everybody talks of peace without realizing,
The opposite of war is not peace, it's unselfishness.
So stop worrying about the fall of civilization.
Live as human so that there actually is a civilization.

Sonnet 66

Civilization doesn't fall from the sky,
Nor is it born in the Capitol building.
The cornerstones of civilized behavior,
Are born of a character that is willing.
Civilization and degradation are born of us,
So far we've been causing degradation.
In a blind pursuit of endless revenue,
We've confused inflation with civilization.
The prime problem with the world is,
All want freedom but not accountability.
That's how vampires in suits and uniforms,
Sell segregation in the name of sovereignty.
Life comes first, then the stars and stripes,
If needed, hundred union jacks be sacrificed.

Sonnet 67

Flags on poles depict savage life,
A life civilized knows no flagmania.
Time for nationalism is long gone,
It's time to stand as one family together.
If we must pledge allegiance,
Let us pledge it to people in need.
Forget King James and Uncle Sam,
As humans and for humans let us live.
If we can lift even five lives,
Then only can we be called human.
One who contains the world in their chest,
Is the one and only civilized person.
While fools entertain hindrances to humanity,
Blood of the civilized boils at the sight of brutality.

24. Bickering and Brokenness
(Sonnet 68 - 70)

Sonnet 68

In our so-called modern world,
Suits and brutes often go together.
People try to hide their heart's dirt,
With clean clothes and fancy manner.
If manner and fashion made human being,
All things concrete would have a golden touch.
Structure of our shelters has changed a lot,
Structure of our heart not so much.
In our walk and talk we may seem civilized,
Inside we are crawling with primeval tendencies.
But that's not really the problem here,
Real problem is our denial of these primitivities.
To be civilized we must break the spell of perfection,
For civilization is born out of willful self-correction.

Sonnet 69

Eraser is not for one who makes mistakes,
Eraser is for the one willing to correct those.
Wise is not the one who wins always,
Wise is the one who knows where to lose.
Cultured is not the one who is learned,
Cultured is the one who's above sectarianism.
Glue is not for one who breaks something,
Glue is for the one willing to fix them.
Joy doesn't come to those chasing joy,
Joy comes to those who live for a purpose.
Life doesn't come to those being reckless,
Life unfolds in the acts of the selfless.
We are all broken one way or another.
Instead of bickering, let's be strength to each other.

Sonnet 70

When we strengthen another,
We become strong ourselves.
When we make another smile,
We become happy ourselves.
When we reach down to lift another,
We lift up ourselves.
When we break ourselves to help another,
Own brokenness is healed by itself.
When we are kind for no reason,
We act as the human we ought to be.
When we lose the self in helping another,
We regain the self with honor and glory.
Key to your life is in another's heart.
To unfold existence disregard all reward.

25. Heaven, Hell and Society
(Sonnet 71 - 73)

Sonnet 71

Regard for reward ruins the heart,
Regard for praise hampers growth.
Live with kindness for kindness is life,
Throw all argumentation overboard.
Mind and mind are not really separate,
They are the streams of one soul.
Streams born of mortal neurons,
Capable of realizing the immortal goal.
All goals are mortal except one,
The eternal dream of collective ascension.
Vegetables may sleep all they want,
Bravehearts must rise without hesitation.
Beyond sleep, security and nonchalance,
There's a valley of, by and for the humans.

Sonnet 72

Sonnet of Heaven and Hell

There's a tale we hear of a heavenly kingdom,
Which is passed on through generations.
Because once you place salvation outside life,
Accountability vanishes from all prioritization.
Self-determination makes one unfit for slavery,
Reason makes one unfit for manipulation.
If you take charge of your life and community,
Institutions fail to dictate your ambition.
Heaven and hell exist here and now,
They are manifestations of human behavior.
Acts of oneness bring heaven in a moment,
Deeds of division breed hell from thin air.
The paradigm we have was made yesterday.
It is our world, let's build it our way.

Sonnet 73

The world is our family,
Our family is our responsibility.
Policy, constitution, bible all later,
First the individual must practice integrity.
Every generation needs caretakers,
The caretaker of your generation is you.
Defying all talks of destiny and success,
Give up yourself to build the society anew.
Let the windbags shout all they want,
You do your existential duty in silence.
Neither woke, nor activist, just as human,
Stand tall with dignity and act with sapience.
The society is ours, so are its troubles.
Walk as the only human amongst vegetables.

26. Wholeness and Tribals
(Sonnet 74 - 76)

Sonnet 74

What makes a human, what makes inhuman,
How can we make the distinction?
Action and expansion make the human,
Inhumans thrive on comfort and contraction.
If your humanity is alive and awake,
You'll despise comfort at the sight of disparity.
If you are not a self-centric inhuman,
You'll be unable to sleep till you lift society.
Luxury lures the shallow and the vain,
Snobs are lost forever in chasing products.
Human beings with backbone and insight,
Cannot be coaxed by separatist constructs.
Civilization awakens when we traverse duality.
Each of us is to be the incarnate of nonduality.

Sonnet 75

Nonduality comes from wholeness,
Wholeness rises when sectarianism is slashed.
Sectarianism fails when we fall in love,
Not with one person but the whole world.
When the stranger becomes family,
Politicians will lose their job.
When love overwhelms all rigidity,
Arms dealers will mourn and sob.
When diplomacy keeps the world divided,
Reliance on institutions goes through the roof.
The best way to sustain profits of war,
Is to keep people infected with the nationalist flu.
Enough with this barbarianism of sovereignty!
Step up and shout, the whole world is my family!

Sonnet 76

In the old days tribal chiefs used to fool people,
With talks of tribal honor and heritage.
Today's chiefs in suits manipulate modern tribals,
With talks of national security and lineage.
When our ancestors behaved as tribals,
It is acceptable for they didn't know better.
But when we identify as civilized yet act tribal,
It is but a degrading stain upon our honor.
Though all politicians are not savages,
Paradigm of modern politics thrives on division.
So make not the dreadful mistake to think,
That politicians are gonna bring peace and elevation.
It is a world of citizens, citizens are its lifeblood.
You and I are its caretakers, not some elected vanguard.

27. Coward Heart (Sonnet 77 - 79)

Sonnet 77

Blaming politicians achieves nothing,
It only enables new crooks and thugs.
Blaming the system achieves nothing,
If you continue as selfish bugs.
It's not enough to thank the soldiers,
Each of us must be the soldier.
It's not enough to thank the martyrs,
Each of us must be the martyr.
Put your thankfulness to some good use,
By taking up responsibility for parts of society.
It's okay if you can't lift the whole world,
At least stand up to your local atrocity.
Law is only the secondary pathway to justice,
The primary path is abolition of cowardice.

Sonnet 78

O my coward heart,
Enough with this cowardice!
When will you beat for real,
Enough with being fear's accomplice!
Your work is to aid life,
Your work is to aid the world.
If you can't do none of that,
Why do you exist at all!
Long you've slept with indifference,
Long you've crawled as vermin.
It is time to stand tall with dignity,
It is time to be a force upliftin'.
O my coward heart, be coward no more,
You've been a doormat enough, now be a lovedoor!

Sonnet 79

There's a door from my heart to yours,
But you can't see it with naked eye.
To see the door from heart to heart,
To all stereotypes you must first die.
There are biases in us that are evolutionary,
Then there are those imposed by culture.
In unlearning these predominant tendencies,
We become humanity's true keeper.
Spare the biases spoil the society,
This is what I once said before.
Biases keep us from becoming human,
We can't be slaves to them no more.
The door of love is opened with love.
Let's open our doors and be the living dove.

28. Blood, Water and Family
(Sonnet 80 - 82)

Sonnet 80

The dove of peace is no mythical creature,
For each of us is a potential dove.
We are the twig and we are the bird,
All peace begins with a human of love.
Mind is the master of war and peace,
Mind is the creator as well as ravager.
Individual will determines collective destiny,
Intention is civilization's true mother.
Diplomacy will not bring peace,
Neither will science and technology.
If the everyday human has no universality,
All power practically breeds insanity.
Nuts and bolts don't make a species advanced.
We are advanced when we walk hand in hand.

Sonnet 81

Sonnet of Blood and Water

Blood may be thicker than water,
But water is far greater than blood.
Blood may discriminate between people,
Water saves all without a single word.
Even while helping the wounded,
Blood discriminates both in mind and medicine.
But to put out the fire of someone's thirst,
Water doesn't care about a single thing.
Now tell me which one deserves all the glory,
Tell me which one is greater,
Is it blood that's prejudiced all the time,
Or is it the life-giving water?
All care for blood and family first,
Few can make a family out of the world.

Sonnet 82

Whatever makes a human being,
Is also what makes a family.
There's no such thing as a stranger,
For a human being with humanity.
All the world is our next of kin,
All towns are our hometown.
There is no my country your country,
All nations are our playground.
Troubles of one are troubles of all,
We are but keepers of each other.
Joy of one is the joy of all,
In helping another our sorrows disappear.
Let us be a boon in each other's life.
Let us be brave and stand together upright.

29. Brain, Body and Being
(Sonnet 83 - 85)

Sonnet 83

Where the head is without fear,
And the heart is without hate,
Where the spine doesn't quiver,
And the feet do not shake,
Where conviction doesn't mind,
The hailstorms of mockery,
Where conscience doesn't retreat,
In vain complacency,
Where character doesn't bow,
Before the myth of authority,
Where life doesn't stoop,
At every whim of primitivity,
Come meet me there at your own pace,
I shall wait for you till my dying days.

Sonnet 84

You don't die when your body dies,
You ain't born when your body is born.
The body and being are not the same,
But they can be if we truly want.
Birth of a brain is birth of potential,
Birth of a brain is birth of possibility.
It doesn't necessarily mean birth of a being,
It doesn't necessarily mean birth of humanity.
CNS holds the seeds of civilization,
Neurons hold the seeds of human living.
But without the will to sow those seeds,
It is just an empty body without a being.
Birth of human is quintessential for global serenity.
Put the animal to sleep and wake up to humanity.

Sonnet 85

Ahoy my friend, wake up to humanity,
Enough with the sleep of tradition!
Be bold, brave and insane if necessary,
And throw overboard all caution.
Don't take travel tips from couch potatoes,
Don't hear tales of revolution from cowards.
Break free from the cocoon of convenience,
Be the one whom inhumanity fears.
Be the pillar the society lacks,
Be the shade for tired pedestrians.
Be the bridge that unites lands,
Be the gate to the earthly heavens.
Distance between lands will all disappear,
With kindness if you can walk up to your neighbor.

30. Love, Hanukkah and Christmas
(Sonnet 86 - 88)

Sonnet 86

Love is Not A Christian Thing
(The Sonnet)

Love thy neighbor is not a christian thing,
Love stuck in barriers stays love no more.
Shalom, ahava, simcha are not jewish concepts,
Peace, love and joy constitute life's core.
There's no christianity, there's only love,
There's no buddhism, there's only compassion,
There's no naskarism, there's only humanity,
There's no humanism, there's only assimilation.
Faith that raises walls within the mind,
Is faith of the prehistoric savages.
Faith has a place in civilized society,
Only if it helps break assumptions and barriers.
Let us come together across faith and culture.
Let us be companions in each other's adventure.

Sonnet 87

Hanukkah Sonnet

Hanukkah, Oh Hanukkah, let's light the menorah,
Let's wipe out all divide, even if some call it utopia.
Come one, come all, no matter the culture,
Let's stuff some latkes while we dreidel together.
Worry not about the candles burning low,
Fear not the darkness of hate and narrowness.
So long as we stand as bridges and not walls,
No darkness is match for our uplifting radiance.
The light of the festival doesn't come from candles,
The sweetness in the air doesn't come from treats.
The light and sweetness of these joyful festivities,
Rise from the loving streams of our heartbeats.
Let us burn bright as the gentle epitome of ahava.
Let us live life as a walking and talking menorah.

Sonnet 88

Christmas Sonnet

Jingle bells, jingle bells, jingle all the way,
Oh, what fun it is to give our own life away!
Saint Nicholas did his part, so did Chris himself,
Now it's time for us to be the happiness gateway.
Dashing through the alleys devoid of lights,
Holding up high as beacon, our own heart,
Breaking ourselves to pieces and burning to ashes,
We'll ensure no one lacks the love a human deserves.
We are Dasher, Dancer, Prancer, Vixen and Comet,
We are Cupid, Donner, Blitzen and Rudolph.
We are also modern day Nick, Chris and Eckhart,
By our love and oneness let the world be engulfed!
Twelve days ain't enough to celebrate Christmas.
As humans we must live each day helping others.

31. Welfare, Politics and Idealism
(Sonnet 89 - 91)

Sonnet 89

One human's despair is all humans' despair,
One human's welfare is all humans' welfare.
When we genuinely start to feel this way,
No neighborhood will be left without care.
There's no politics, there's only accountability,
There's no equity, there's only sanity.
There's no diversity, there's only life,
There's no rights, there's only humanity.
Party is just a means of change,
Meant to bring reform through organization.
But in reality party takes preference over people,
And becomes the problem instead of the solution.
Use your neurons and defy all political histrionics.
Build a society that requires no party politics.

Sonnet 90

Sonnet of The Benevolent Crook

Politics doesn't mean affairs of the people,
It is but a telenovela of sectarian histrionics.
Democracy doesn't mean rule of the people,
It means a new dictatorship of the charismatic.
A paradigm born of selfishness and greed,
Is no place for an honest and innocent person.
But if politics is the path you choose for reform,
Leave theories outside before entering the dungeon.
When you are compelled to be crooked,
Make sure it is not for any benefit personal.
Be the Godfather of crookedness if needed,
And manipulate the system to lift the people.
All abuse power of politics to climb the social ladder.
Be the benevolent crook and use it as social leveler.

Sonnet 91

Idealism has no place in an organic world,
It only hampers the growth of humanity.
No matter how perfect their bookish definition is,
In the real world they all function differently.
Sometimes I shake hands with the devil,
Sometimes I am the devil myself.
If you are crooked to the hypocrites for people,
The end does justify the means quite well.
I ain't no diplomat, I ain't no scholar,
I am but a simple soul off the street.
Based on the requirement of the situation,
I'll do whatever it takes to ensure social uplift.
It is a hypocrites' world where honesty is a curse.
Though gentle inside, learn to pretend dangerous.

32. Honesty and Luxury
(Sonnet 92 - 94)

Sonnet 92

They say honesty is the best policy,
Because honest cowards make ideal slaves.
If you have a backbone and you use your brain,
Crooked overlords lose their authoritative reins.
It's good for corruption to have law-abiding citizens,
Who are complacent and pay disparities no heed.
Original thinking makes one unfit for exploitation,
Corruption thrives on people's endless greed.
When people start to feel, think and act as human,
They will be silent less and will stand up more.
When they start to live as beings of character,
They will buy things less and help others more.
There is no best policy till that policy applies to all.
What matters is, we are responsible for our world.

Sonnet 93

Enough with blaming the bureaucrats,
Enough with blaming the politicians.
The regular civilians are no better,
In fact, they are worse than the authoritarians.
For trivial things they shout at the lowly,
At real inhumanities they keep quiet.
Over coffee they debate law and policy,
While living life as corruption incarnate.
Billion dollar scams are not the only scam,
A dollar worth of greed is also crime.
Corruption does not fall from the sky above,
Civilian corruption is the root of it all every time.
Uncorrupt democracy is born of uncorrupt civilians.
Before you blame a politician, observe your actions.

Sonnet 94

Dollar of Disparity

(The Sonnet)

Millions of people go without food,
For some privileged nimrods to afford their luxuries.
Millions of people have no access to essentials,
So that celebrities can buy their lamborghinis.
The difference between phony activists and a reformer,
Is not in what they say but in their lifestyle and action.
In a world that still suffers from the lack of essentials,
Indulgence in luxury is human rights violation.
What people do with their money is not a private affair,
Each penny above necessity belongs to social welfare.
One who talks of equality while riding in a Rolls Royce,
Is the last person to be concerned of people's despair.
None has a right to luxury till all can access necessities.
Every dollar spent on luxury is a dollar of disparity.

33. Behavior and Oneness
(Sonnet 95 - 97)

Sonnet 95

Divisionism and dollarism are the curse of society,
Yet society worships them as the greatest boon.
Peace and peoplism are cussed as commie claptrap,
While populism continues to give power to goons.
No society is born just, warm and humane,
It falls upon each of us to shape it in such a way.
You don't need to run for office to bring reform,
You just need to stop brushing your duties away.
Not all politicians are reformers,
Though every single one of them pretends to be.
But every responsible civilian is living reformation,
Even if they do not say anything to anybody.
Reformation is not a matter of brainless partisanism,
It is a matter of nonpartisan and hearty collectivism.

Sonnet 96

The sun doesn't call itself light-bringer,
Yet the whole world venerates it as such.
The wind doesn't call itself the soother,
Yet the whole world craves for its gush.
The rivers don't call themselves life-giver,
Yet the world can't function without their currents.
The reformer doesn't call themselves humanizer,
Yet all progress comes to halt without their footsteps.
If someone identifies as a scientist or humanist,
It means nothing till they use science to lift others.
If someone identifies as an activist or humanitarian,
It means nothing till they can be annihilated for others.
Designation-dropping is habit of the kindergartener.
Identity of grownups is revealed through behavior.

Sonnet 97

Age doesn't make you wise, curiosity does.
Intellect doesn't make you curious, growth does.
Experience doesn't make you grow, expansion does.
Travel doesn't make you expand, self-correction does.
Cynicism doesn't help correction, awareness does.
Books don't make you aware, accountability does.
Law cannot make you accountable, humanity does.
Appearance doesn't make you human, acceptance does.
Wokeness doesn't make you accepting, character does.
Clothes don't make character, conduct does.
Etiquettes don't define conduct, goodness does.
Tradition doesn't make you good, oneness does.
Oneness is the mother of all civilized behavior.
Without oneness we're ever headed for disaster.

34. Success and Commencement
(Sonnet 98 – 100)

Sonnet 98

There's no humanity,
Only degrees of animality.
There's no civility,
Only degrees of primitivity.
We are not even close,
To be worthy of the title human.
All we can do however,
Is be less of an animal.
It is not rocket science,
Just a matter of willfulness.
Are you willful enough,
To defy your innate selfishness!
Bold steps without self-regulation,
Like cancer, ultimately causes destruction.

Sonnet 99

Self-regulation is not caution,
It is an act of course-correction.
Too much sentiment and no reason,
Destroys both the path and the pedestrian.
Be aware of your shortcomings,
As well as your greatest strength.
Adjust the means and pace of your course,
Thinking as a whole being with heart and head.
There is no surefire way to success,
Success and failure are products of capitalist torment.
Life is but an experiment of trial and error,
Instead of fretting the future, cherish the experiment.
If today's you is slightly more human than yesterday,
That is true success, no matter what creeplings say.

Sonnet 100

If success makes you cold and apathetic,
Better be unsuccessful and suffer every day.
If materials imprison you in a castle of cockiness,
Better live simple and keep all luxuries at bay.
If intellect makes you distant from the people,
Better be dumb and exude a ton of humility.
If power makes you corrupt like everybody else,
Better stay away from positions of authority.
Tribalism and self-centricity are universal,
So are the abilities of awareness and moderation.
What is not universal in this whole wide world,
Is the practice of those abilities of civilization.
It's a blunderful world and humankind is the cause of it.
No matter the history, let us commence operation fixit.

BIBLIOGRAPHY

Archer M., (2000), Being Human: The Problem of Agency. Cambridge University Press.

Adolphs R (2003) Cognitive neuroscience of human social behaviour. Nature Rev Neurosci 4: 165–178.

Adolphs R, Tranel D, Damasio AR (2003) Dissociable neural systems for recognizing emotions. Brain Cogn 52: 61–69.

Andresen, Jensine, and Robert Forman, eds. Cognitive Models and Spiritual Maps. Bowling Green, Ohio: Imprint Academic, 2000.

Azari, Nina, Janpeter Nickel, Gilbert Wunderlich, Michael Niedeggen, Harald Hefter, Lutz Tellmann, Hans Herzog, Petra Stoerig, Dieter Birnbacher, and Rudiger Seitz. "Neural Correlates of Religious Experience."

European Journal of Neuroscience 13, no. 8 (2001)

Agar, N. (2004). Liberal eugenics: In defence of human enhancement. London: Blackwell Publishing.

Alteheld, N., Roessler, G., Vobig, M., & Walter, R. (2004). The retina implant new approach to a visual prosthesis. Biomedizinische Technik, 49(4), 99–103.

Antal, A., Nitsche, M. A., Kincses, T. Z., Kruse, W., Hoffmann, K. P., & Paulus, W. (2004a). Facilitation of visuo-motor learning by transcranial direct current stimulation of the motor and extrastriate visual areas in humans. European Journal of Neuroscience, 19(10), 2888–2892.

Bernstein R.J., (1971), Praxis and Action: Contemporary Philosophies of Human Activity. Philadelphia: University of Pennsylvania Press.

Bernstein R.J., (1976), The Restructuring Social and Political Thought.

Bernstein R.J., (1983), Beyond Relativism and Objectivism: Science, Hermeneutics, and Praxis. Philadelphia: University of Pennsylvania Press.

Bernstein R.J., (1986), Philosophical Profiles. Philadelphia: University of Pennsylvania Press.

Bernstein R.J., (1991), New Constellation. Cambridge: MIT Press.

Birkhead, T. R., Johnson, S. D. & Nettleship, D. N. (1985). Extra-pair matings and mate guarding in the common murre Uria aalge. - Anim. Behav. 33, p. 608-619.

Beauregard, Mario, and Vincent Paquette. "Neural Correlates of a Mystical Experience in Carmelite Nuns." Neuroscience Letters 405, no. 3 (2006)

Benson, Herbert. Timeless Healing: The Power and Biology of Belief. New York: Scribner, 1996

Bose, Subhas Chandra. An Indian Pilgrim: An Unfinished Autobiography, Oxford University Press, 1997

Bogen, J.E.(1995a), 'On the neurophysiology of consciousness: Part I. An overview', Consciousness and Cognition, 4.

Bogen, J.E. (1995b), 'On the neurophysiology of consciousness: Part II. Constraining the semantic problem', Consciousness and Cognition, 4.

Bremner, J. D., R. Soufer, et al. (2001). "Gender differences in cognitive and neural correlates of remembrance of emotional words." Psychopharmacol Bull 35 (3).

Brothers, L. (2002). The social brain: A project for integrating primate behavior and neurophysiology in a new domain. In J. T. Cacioppo et al. (Eds.), Foundations in neuroscience. Cambridge, MA: MIT Press.

Buss, D. D. (2003). Evolutionary Psychology: The New Science of Mind, 2nd ed. New York: Allyn & Bacon.

Buss, D. M. (1989). "Conflict between the sexes: Strategic interference and the evocation of anger and upset." J Pers Soc Psychol 56 (5).

Buss, D. M. (1995). "Psychological sex differences. Origins through sexual selection." Am Psychol 50 (3).

Buss, D. M., and D. P. Schmitt (1993). "Sexual strategies theory: An evolutionary perspective on human mating." Psychol Rev 100 (2).

Blakemore SJ, Decety J (2001) From the perception of action to the understanding of intention. Nature Rev Neurosci 2: 561.

Colapietro V., (1988), "Human Agency: The Habits of Our Being." Southern Journal of Philosophy, XXVI, 2, pp. 153-68.

Colapietro V., (1992), "Purpose, Power, and Agency." The Monist, 75, 4 (October) pp. 423-44.

Colapietro V., (2004a), "C. S. Peirce's Reclamation of Teleology." Nature in American Philosophy, ed. Jean De Groot (Washington, D.C.: Catholic University Press of America), pp. 88-108.

Carey DP, Perrett DI, Oram MW (1997) Recognizing, understanding and reproducing actions. In: Jeannerod M, Grafman J (eds) Handbook of neuropsychology. Vol. 11: Action and cognition. Elsevier, Amsterdam.

Carr L, Iacoboni M, Dubeau MC, Mazziotta JC, Lenzi GL (2003) Neural mechanisms of empathy in humans: a relay from neural systems for imitation to limbic areas. Proc Natl Acad Sci USA 100: 5497–5502.

Chomsky Noam, (2017) Requiem for the American Dream

Chomsky Noam, (2016) Who Rules the World?

Chomsky Noam, (2010) How the World Works

Churchland, P.S. (1986), Neurophilosophy (Cambridge, MA: The MIT Press).

Churchland, P.S. & Ramachandran, V.S. (1993), 'Filling in: Why Dennett is wrong', in Dennett and His Critics: Demystifying Mind, ed. B. Dahlbom (Oxford: Blackwell Scientific Press).

Churchland, P.S., Ramachandran, V.S. & Sejnowski, T.J. (1994), 'A critique of pure vision', in Large- scale Neuronal Theories of the Brain, ed. C. Koch & J.L. Davis (Cambridge, MA: The MIT Press).

Coyle EF. Integration of the physiological factors determining endurance performance ability. Exerc Sport Sci Rev. 1995;23:25–63.

Crick, F. (1994), The Astonishing Hypothesis: The Scientific Search for the Soul (New York: Simon and Schuster).

Crick, F. (1996), 'Visual perception: rivalry and consciousness', Nature, 379.

Crick, F. & Koch, C. (1992), 'The problem of consciousness', Scientific American, 267.

Damasio, A (2003a) Looking for Spinoza. Harcourt Inc. Damasio A (2003b) Feeling of emotion and the self. Ann NY Acad Sci 1001: 253–261.

d'Aquili, Eugene. "Senses of Reality in Science and Religion." Zygon 17, no 4 (1982)

d'Aquili, Eugene. "The Biopsychological Determinants of Religious Ritual Behavior." Zygon 10, no. 1 (1975)

d'Aquili, Eugene. "The Myth-Ritual Complex: A Biogenetic Structural Analysis." Zygon 18, no. 3 (1983)

d'Aquili, Eugene, and Andrew Newberg. The Mystical Mind: Probing the Biology of Religious Experience. Minneapolis: Fortress Press, 1999.

Daly DD. 1958. Ictal affect. Am J Psychiatry.

Damasio, A. (1994) Descartes' Error: Emotion, Reason and the Human Brain. New York, Putnams.

Damasio, A. (1999) The Feeling of What Happens: Body, Emotion and the Making of Consciousness. London, Heinemann.

Darwin, C. (1859) On the Origin of Species by Means of Natural Selection. London, Murray.

Darwin, C. (1871) The Descent of Man and Selection in Relation to Sex. London, John Murray.

Darwin, C. (1872) The Expression of the Emotions in Man and Animals. London, John Murray; also published 1965, Chicago, University of Chicago Press.

Dawkins, M.S. (1987) Minding and mattering. In C. Blakemore and S. Greenfield (eds) Mindwaves. Oxford, Blackwell, 151-60.

Dawkins, R. (1976) The Selfish Gene. Oxford, Oxford University Press; a new edition, with additional material, was published in 1989.

Di Pellegrino G, Fadiga L, Fogassi L, Gallese V, Rizzolatti G (1992) Understanding motor events: A neurophysiological study. Exp Brain Res 91: 176–80.

Deikman, A.J. (2000) A functional approach to mysticism. Journal of Consciousness Studies 7(11-12), 75-91.

Delmonte, M.M. (1987) Personality and meditation. In M. West (ed.) The Psychology of Meditation. Oxford, Clarendon Press, 118-32.

Dennett, D.C. (1988) Quining qualia. In A.J. Marcel and E. Bisiach (eds) Consciousness in Contemporary Science. Oxford, Oxford University Press, 42-77.

Dennett, D.C. (1991) Consciousness Explained. Boston, MA, and London, Little, Brown and Co.

Dennett, D.C. (1995a) Darwin's Dangerous Idea. London, Penguin.

Dennett, D.C. (1998b) Brainchildren: Essays on Designing Minds. Cambridge, MA, MIT Press.

Dewhurst, Kenneth, and A. W. Beard. "Sudden Religious Conversions in Temporal Lobe Epilepsy." British Journal of Psychiatry 117 (1970)

Dewhurst K, Beard AW. Sudden religious conversions in temporal lobe epilepsy. 1970 Epilepsy Behav 2003

Devinsky O, Lai G. Spirituality and religion in epilepsy. Epilepsy Behav 2008.

Devinsky, O., Morrell, MJ, Vogt, BA. (1995) 'Contribution of anterior cingulate cortex to behavior', Brain, 118.

E. Horvitz, "One Hundred Year Study on Artificial Intelligence: Reflections and Framing," ed: Stanford University, 2014.

Eckhart Meister, Selected Writings

Egidi R., ed. (1999), "Von Wright and 'Dante's Dream': Stages in a Philosophical Pilgrim's Progress", in

In Search of a New Humanism: the Philosophy of G.H. von Wright, ed. by R. Egidi, Kluwer, Dordrecht.

Fadiga L, Fogassi L, Pavesi G, Rizzolatti G (1995) Motor facilitation during action observation: a magnetic stimulation study. J Neurophysiol 73: 2608–2611.

Fogassi L, Gallese V, Fadiga L, Rizzolatti G (1998) Neurons responding to the sight of goal directed hand/arm actions in the parietal area PF (7b) of the macaque monkey. Soc Neurosci Abs 24:257.5.

Frith U, Frith CD (2003) Development and neurophysiology of mentalizing. Philos Trans R Soc Lond B Biol Sci 358: 459.

Farah, M.J. (1989), 'The neural basis of mental imagery', Trends in Neurosciences, 10.

Finlay BL, Darlington RB (1995) Linked regularities in the development and evolution of mammalian brains. Science 268.

Freud, S. "The Interpretation of Dreams", 1900

Freud, S. "Selected papers on hysteria and other psychoneuroses" Journal of Nervous and Mental Disease 1909.

Freud, S. "The Origin and Development of Psychoanalysis", 1910

Freud, S. "Psychopathology of everyday life", 1914

Freud, S. "Beyond the Pleasure Principle", 1920

Frith, C.D. & Dolan, R.J. (1997), 'Abnormal beliefs: Delusions and memory', Paper presented at the May, 1997, Harvard Conference on Memory and Belief.

Gay, Volney, ed. Neuroscience and Religion. Plymouth, UK: Lexington Books, 2009.

Gazzaniga, M. S. (1985). The social brain. New York: Basic Books.

Gazzaniga, M.S. (1993), 'Brain mechanisms and conscious experience', Ciba Foundation Symposium, 174.

Geschwind N. "Behavioural changes in temporal lobe epilepsy". Psychol Med. 1979.

Gellhorn, E., Kiely, W.F. "Mystical states of consciousness: neurophysiological and clinical aspects." J Nerv Ment Dis. 1972;154:399-405.

Gilbert SL, Dobyns WB, Lahn BT (2005) Genetic links between brain development and brain evolution. Nat Rev Genet 6.

Gray JA. The Psychology of Fear and Stress. 2nd ed. New York, NY: Cambridge University Press; 1988.

Gloor, P. (1992), 'Amygdala and temporal lobe epilepsy', in The Amygdala: Neurobiological Aspects of Emotion, Memory and Mental Dysfunction, ed J.P. Aggleton (New York: Wiley-Liss).

Greenspan, S. I. and S. G. Shanker (2004). The first idea: How symbols, language, and intelligence evolved from our early primate ancestors to modern humans. Cambridge, MA: Da Capo Press.

Grady, D. (1993), 'The vision thing: Mainly in the brain', Discover, June.

Gallagher HL, Frith CD (2003) Functional imaging of 'theory of mind'. Trends Cogn Sci 7: 77.

Gallese V, Fogassi L, Fadiga L, Rizzolatti G (2002) Action representation and the inferior parietal lobule. In: Prinz W, Hommel B (eds) Attention & Performance XIX. Common mechanisms in perception and action. Oxford University Press, Oxford.

Gallese V, Keysers C, Rizzolatti G (2004) A unifying view of the basis of social cognition. Trends Cogn Sci 8: 396–403.

Goldman AI, Sripada CS (2004) Simulationist models of face-based emotion recognition. Cognition 94: 193–213.

Grèzes J, Costes N, Decety J (1998) Top-down effect of strategy on the perception of human biological motion: a PET investigation. Cogn Neuropsychol 15: 553–582.

Grèzes J, Armony JL, Rowe J, Passingham RE (2003) Activations related to "mirror" and "canonical" neurones in the human brain: an fMRI study. Neuroimage 18: 928–937.

Gross CG, Rocha-Miranda CE, Bender DB (1972) Visual properties of neurons in the inferotemporal cortex of the macaque. J Neurophysiol 35: 96–111.

Guevara Che, The Motorcycle Diaries, 1992

Hari R, Forss N, Avikainen S, Kirveskari S, Salenius S, Rizzolatti G (1998) Activation of human primary motor cortex during action observation: a neuromagnetic study. Proc. Natl Acad Sci USA 95: 15061–15065.

Hardy, G. H. (1940). Ramanujan. Cambridge: Cambridge University Press.

Hall, Daniel, Keith Meador, and Harold Koenig. "Measuring Religiousness in Health Research: Review and Critique." Journal of Religion and Health 47, no. 2 (2008)

Harris, Sam, Jonas Kaplan, Ashley Curiel, Susan Bookheimer, Marco Iacoboni, and Mark Cohen. "The Neural Correlates of Religious and

Nonreligious Belief." PLoS One 4, no. 10 (October 1, 2009)

Halgren, E. (1992), 'Emotional neurophysiology of the amygdala within the context of human cognition', in The Amygdala: Neurobiological Aspects of Emotion, Memory and Mental Dysfunction, ed J.P. Aggleton (New York: Wiley-Liss).

Halligan PW, Fink GR, Marshal JC, Vallar G. 2003. Spatial cognition: evidence from visual neglect. Trends Cogn Sci.

Handbook of Emotions, Edited by Michael Lewis, Jeannette M. Haviland-Jones, and Lisa Feldman Barrett, The Guilford Press; 3rd edition (2010).

Hameroff, S.R. and Penrose, R. (1996) Conscious events as orchestrated space-time selections. Journal of Consciousness Studies 3(1), 36-53; also reprinted in J. Shear (ed.) (1997) Explaining Consciousness-The Hard

Problem. Cambridge, MA, MIT Press, 177-95.

Harding, D.E. (1961) On Having no Head: Zen and the Re-Discovery of the Obvious. London, Buddhist Society.

Hardy, A. (1979) The Spiritual Nature of Man: A Study of Contemporary Religious Experience. Oxford, Clarendon Press.

Harre, R. and Gillett, G. (1994) The Discursive Mind. Thousand Oaks, CA, Sage.

Haugeland, J. (ed.) (1997) Mind Design II: Philosophy, Psychology, Artificial Intelligence. Cambridge, MA, MIT Press.

Hauser, M.D. (2000) Wild Minds: What Animals Really Think. New York, Henry Holt and Co.; London, Penguin.

Hebb, D.O. (1949) The Organization of Behavior. New York, Wiley.

Helmholtz, H.L.F. von (1856-67) Treatise on Physiological Optics.

Hess, EH (1975) "The role of pupil size in communication," Scientific American, 233(5), 110–12.

Heyes, C.M. (1998) Theory of mind in nonhuman primates. Behavioral and Brain Sciences 21, 101-48; with commentaries.

Heyes, C.M. and Galef, B.G. (eds) (1996) Social Learning in Animals: The Roots of Culture. San Diego, CA, Academic Press.

Hilgard, E.R. (1986) Divided Consciousness: Multiple Controls in Human Thought and Action. New York, Wiley.

Hilton, E.N., Lundberg, T.R. Transgender Women in the Female Category of Sport: Perspectives on Testosterone Suppression and Performance Advantage. Sports Med 51, 199–214 (2021).

Hitler, Adolf. Mein Kampf, 1925

Hodgson, R. (1891) A case of double consciousness. Proceedings of the Society for Psychical Research 7, 221-58.

Hofstadter, D.R. and Dennett, D.C. (eds) (1981) The Mind's I: Fantasies and Reflections on Self and Soul. London, Penguin.

Holland, J. (ed.) (2001) Ecstasy: The Complete Guide: A Comprehensive Look at the Risks and Benefits of MDMA. Rochester, VT, Park Street Press.

Holmes, D.S. (1987) The influence of meditation versus rest on physiological arousal. In M. West (ed.) The Psychology of Meditation. Oxford, Clarendon Press, 81-103.

Holmstrom, David. 1992, Christian Science Monitor

Holt, J. (1999) Blindsight in debates about qualia. Journal of Consciousness Studies 6(5), 54-71.

Holloway RL (1996) Evolution of the human brain. In: Lock A, Peters CR (eds) Handbook of human symbolic evolution. Oxford University Press, Oxford

Iacoboni M, Woods RP, Brass M, Bekkering H, Mazziotta JC, Rizzolatti G (1999) Cortical mechanisms of human imitation. Science 286: 2526–2528.

Iacoboni M, Koski LM, Brass M, Bekkering H, Woods RP, Dubeau MC, Mazziotta JC, Rizzolatti G (2001) Reafferent copies of imitated actions in the right superior temporal cortex. Proc Natl Acad Sci USA 98: 13995–13999.

Jeannerod M (1988) The neural and behavioural organization of goal-directed movements. Clarendon Press, Oxford.

Johnson-Frey SH, Maloof FR, Newman-Norlund R, Farrer C, Inati S, Grafton ST (2003) Actions or hand-objects interactions? Human inferior frontal cortex and action observation. Neuron 39: 1053–1058.

Jackson, F. (1982) Epiphenomenal qualia. Philosophical Quarterly 32, 127-36.

James, W. (1890) The Principles of Psychology (2 volumes). London, Macmillan.

James, W. (1902) The Varieties of Religious Experience: A Study in Human Nature. New York and London, Longmans, Green and Co.

Jansen, K. (2001) Ketamine: Dreams and Realities. Sarasota, FL, Multidisciplinary Association for Psychedelic Studies.

Jay, M. (ed.) (1999) Artificial Paradises: A Drugs Reader. London, Penguin.

Jaynes, J. (1976) The Origin of Consciousness in the Breakdown of the Bicameral Mind. New York, Houghton Mifflin.

Johnson, M.K. and Raye, C.L. (1981) Reality monitoring. Psychological Review 88, 67-85.

Kadim I, Mahgoub O, Baqir S et al. (2015) Cultured meat from muscle stem cells: a review of challenges and prospects. J Integr Agr 14: 222–233

Kandel, E. R. In Search of Memory: The Emergence of a New Science of Mind, W. W. Norton & Company (2007).

Kandel E. R. Schwartz JH, Jessel TM. Principles of neural sciences. New York; McGraw Hill, 2000.

Kanwisher, N. (2001) Neural events and perceptual awareness. Cognition

79, 89-113; also reprinted inS. Dehaene (ed.) The Cognitive Neuroscience of Consciousness. Cambridge, MA, MIT Press, 89-113.

Karn, K. and Hayhoe, M. (2000) Memory representations guide targeting eye movements in a natural task. Visual Cognition 7, 673-703.

Kennedy, H., & Dehay, C. (1988). Functional implications of the anatomical organization of the callosal projections of visual areas V1 and V2 in the macaque monkey. Behav. Brain Res., 29, 225–236.

Kentridge, R.W. and Heywood, C.A. (1999) The status of blindsight. Journal of Consciousness Studies 6(5), 3-11.

Kihlstrom, J.F. (1996) Perception without awareness of what is perceived, learning without awareness of what is learned. In M. Velmans (ed.) The Science of Consciousness. London, Routledge, 23-46.

Kosslyn, S.M. (1980) Image and Mind. Cambridge, MA, Harvard University Press.

Kosslyn, S.M. (1988) Aspects of a cognitive neuroscience of mental imagery. Science 240, 1621-6.

Kinsbourne, M. (1995), 'The intralaminar thalamic nucleii', Consciousness and Cognition, 4.

Kjaer, Troels, Camilla Bertelsen, Paola Piccini, David Brooks, Jorgen Alving, and Hans Lou. "Increased Dopamine Tone during Meditation- Induced Change of Consciousness." Cognitive Brain Research 13, no. 2 (April 2002)

Kölmel HW. 1985. Complex visual hallucinations in the hemianopic field. J Neurol Neurosurg Psychiatry.

Koenig, Harold. "Research on Religion, Spirituality, and Mental Health: A Review." Canadian Journal of Psychiatry 54, no. 5 (May 2009)

Koenig, Harold, ed. Handbook of Religion and Mental Health. San Diego, CA: Academic Press, 1998

Kraepelin E. Psychiatry: A Textbook for Students and Physicians. New York, NY: Science History Publications; 1990.

Lauglin, Charles, John McManus, and Eugene d'Aquili. Brain, Symbol, and Experience. 2nd ed. New York: Columbia University Press, 1992

Lakoff, G. and M. Johnson (1999). Philosophy in the flesh. Basic Books: New York.

LeDoux, J. E. (1996). The emotional brain. New York: Simon & Schuster.

LeDoux, J.E. (1992), 'Emotion and the amygdala', in The Amygdala: Neurobiological Aspects of Emo- tion, Memory and Mental Dysfunction, ed J.P. Aggleton (New York: Wiley-Liss).

Levin, D.T. and Simons, D.J. (1997) Failure to detect changes to attended objects in motion pictures. Psychonomic Bulletin and Review 4, 501-6.

Levine,J. (1983) Materialism and qualia: the explanatory gap. Pacific Philosophical Quarterly 64, 354-61.

Levine,J. (2001) Purple Haze: The Puzzle of Consciousness. New York, Oxford University Press. Levine, S. (1979) A Gradual Awakening. New York, Doubleday.

Levinson, B.W. (1965) States of awareness during general anaesthesia. British Journal of Anaesthesia 37, 544-6.

Lewicki, P., Czyzewska, M. and Hoffman, H. (1987) Unconscious acquisition of complex procedural knowledge. Journal of Experimental Psychology: Learning, Memory and Cognition 13, 523-30.

Lewicki, P., Hill, T. and Bizot, E. (1988) Acquisition of procedural knowledge about a pattern of stimuli that cannot be articulated. Cognitive Psychology 20, 24-37.

Lewicki, P., Hill, T. and Czyzewska, M. (1992) Nonconscious acquisition of information. American Psychologist 47, 796-801.

Manthey S, Schubotz RI, von Cramon DY (2003). Premotor cortex in observing erroneous action: an fMRI study. Brain Res Cogn Brain Res 15: 296–307.

Mesulam MM, Mufson EJ (1982) Insula of the old world monkey. III: Efferent cortical output and comments on function. J Comp Neurol 212: 38–52.

Naskar, Abhijit. "Homo: A Brief History of Consciousness", 2015

Naskar, Abhijit. "What is Mind?", 2016

Naskar, Abhijit. "Love, God & Neurons: Memoir of A Scientist who found himself by getting lost", 2016

Naskar, Abhijit. "Principia Humanitas", 2017

Naskar, Abhijit. "We Are All Black: A Treatise on Racism", 2017

Naskar, Abhijit. "Either Civilized or Phobic: A Treatise on Homosexuality", 2017

Naskar, Abhijit. "The Bengal Tigress: A Treatise on Gender Equality", 2017

Naskar, Abhijit. "Morality Absolute", 2017

Naskar, Abhijit. "Build Bridges not Walls: In the name of Americana", 2018

Naskar, Abhijit. "Fabric of Humanity", 2018

Naskar, Abhijit. "Citizens of Peace: Beyond the Savagery of Sovereignty", 2019

Naskar, Abhijit. "The Constitution of The United Peoples of Earth", 2019

Naskar, Abhijit. "Neurons Giveth, Neurons Taketh Away | Abhijit Naskar | TEDxIIMRanchi", 2019 https://www.youtube.com/watch?v=B NX-Q0ySm80

Naskar, Abhijit. "Mission Reality", 2019

Naskar, Abhijit. "Operation Justice: To Make A Society That Needs No Law", 2019

Naskar, Abhijit. "Every Generation Needs Caretakers: The Gospel of Patriotism", 2020

Naskar, Abhijit. "Hurricane Humans: Give me accountability, I'll give you peace", 2020

Naskar, Abhijit. "Revolution Indomable", 2020

Naskar, Abhijit. "Servitude is Sanctitude", 2020

Naskar, Abhijit. "Good Scientist: When Science and Service Combine", 2020

Newberg, Andrew, and Jeremy Iversen. "The Neural Basis of the Complex Mental Task of Meditation: Neurotransmitter and Neurochemical Considerations." Medical Hypotheses 61, no. 2 (2003).

Newberg, Andrew. "How God Changes Your Brain: An Introduction to Jewish Neurotheology", CCAR Journal: The Reform Jewish Quarterly, Winter 2016.

Newberg, Andrew, and Stephanie Newberg. "A Neuropsychological Perspective on Spiritual Development." In Handbook of Spiritual Development in Childhood and Adolescence, edited by Eugene

Roehlkepartain, Pamela King, Linda Wagener, and Peter Benson. London: Sage Publications, Inc., 2005

Newberg, Andrew. "The Neurotheology Link An Intersection Between Spirituality and Health", Alternative and Complimentary Therapies, Vol 21 No 1, February 2015.

Newberg, Andrew, Nancy Wintering, Dharma Khalsa, Hannah Roggenkamp, and Mark Waldman. "Meditation Effects on Cognitive Function and Cerebral Blood Flow in Subjects with Memory Loss: A Preliminary Study." Journal of Alzheimer's Disease 20, no. 2 (2010)

Nash, M. (1995), 'Glimpses of the mind', Time.

Nesse RM. Proximate and evolutionary studies of anxiety, stress and depression: synergy at the interface. Neurosci Biobehav Rev. 1999;23:895-903.

Nicolelis, Miguel. (2011) "Beyond Boundaries: The New Neuroscience of Connecting Brains with Machines---and How It Will Change Our Lives", Times Books

O'Hara, K. and Scutt, T. (1996) There is no hard problem of consciousness. Journal of Consciousness Studies 3(4), 290-302, reprinted in J. Shear (ed.) (1997) Explaining Consciousness. Cambridge, MA, MIT Press, 69-82.

O'Regan, J.K. (1992) Solving the "real" mysteries of visual perception: the world as an outside memory. Canadian Journal of Psychology 46, 461-88.

O'Regan, J.K. and Noe, A. (2001) A sensorimotor account of vision and visual consciousness. Behavioral and Brain Sciences 24(5), 883-917.

O'Regan, J.K., Rensink, R.A. and Clark,].]. (1999) Change-blindness as a result of "mudsplashes." Nature 398, 34.

Ornstein, R.E. (1977) The Psychology of Consciousness (2nd edn). New York, Harcourt.

Ornstein, R.E. (1986) The Psychology of Consciousness (3rd edn). New York, Pehguin.

Ornstein, R.E. (1992) The Evolution of Consciousness. New York, Touchstone.

Penfield W, Faulk ME (1955) The insula: further observations on its function. Brain 78: 445– 470.

Penrose, R. (1994), Shadows of the Mind (Oxford: Oxford University Press).

Penrose, R. (1989), The Emperor's New Mind: Concerning Computers, Minds and The Laws of Physics (Oxford: Oxford University Press).

Persinger, "'I would kill in God's name' role of sex, weekly church attendance, report of a religious experience and limbic lability" Perceptual and Motor Skills 1997.

Persinger "Experimental simulation of the God experience" Neurotheology 2003.

Persinger, Corradini, Clement, Keaney, et al "Neurotheology and its convergence with neuroquantology" NeuroQuantology 2010.

Persinger, Koren and St-Pierre "The electromagnetic induction of mystical and altered states within the laboratory" Journal of Consciousness Exploration and Research 2010.

Persinger "Case report: A prototypical spontaneous 'sensed presence' of a sentient being and concomitant electroencephalographic activity in the clinical laboratory" Neurocase 2008.

Persinger and Saroka "Potential production of Hughlings Jackson's "parasitic consciousness" by physiologically-patterned weak transcerebral magnetic fields: QEEG and source localization" Epilepsy & Behavior 28 (2013).

Persinger. "The neuropsychiatry of paranormal experiences". J Neuropsychiatry Clin Neurosci 2001.

Persinger. "Neuropsychological bases of god beliefs", New York: Praeger, 1987

Persinger. "Temporal lobe epileptic signs and correlative behaviors displayed by normal populations", Journal of General Psychology, 1986

Perry BD, Pollard R. Homeostasis, stress, trauma, and adaptation. A neurodevelopmental view of childhood trauma. Child Adolesc Psychiatr Clin N Am. 1998;7:33.

Paré, D. & Llinás, R. (1995), 'Conscious and preconscious processes as seen from the standpoint of sleep-waking cycle neurophysiology', Neuropsychologia, 33.

Phillips ML, Young AW, Senior C, Brammer M, Andrew C, Calder AJ, Bullmore ET, Perrett DI, Rowland D, Williams SC, Gray JA, David AS (1997) A specific neural substrate for perceiving facial expressions of disgust. Nature 389: 495–498.

Phillips ML, Young AW, Scott SK, Calder AJ, Andrew C, Giampietro V, Williams SC, Bullmore ET, Brammer M, Gray JA (1998) Neural responses to facial and vocal expressions of fear and disgust. Proc R Soc Lond B Biol Sci 265: 1809–1817.

Puce A, Perrett D (2003) Electrophysiological and brain imaging of biological motion. Philosoph Trans Royal Soc Lond, Series B, 358: 435–445.

Ramachandran VS. Behavioral and magnetoencephalographic correlates of plasticity in the adult human brain. Proc Natl Acad Sci USA 1993; 90: 10413–20.

Ramachandran VS. Phantom limbs, neglect syndromes, repressed memories, and Freudian psychology. Int Rev Neurobiol 1994; 37: 291–333.

Ramachandran VS. Plasticity and functional recovery in neurology. Clin Med 2005; 5: 368–73.

Ramachandran VS, Hirstein W. The perception of phantom limbs. The D. O. Hebb lecture. Brain 1998; 121: 1603–30.

Ramachandran VS, Rogers-Ramachandran D, Cobb S. Touching the phantom limb. Nature 1995; 377: 489–90.

Ramachandran VS, Rogers-Ramachandran D. Phantom limbs and

neural plasticity. Arch Neurol 2000; 57: 317–20.

Ramachandran VS, Rogers-Ramachandran D. It's all done with mirrors. Sci Am Mind 2007; 18: 16–9.

Ramachandran VS, Rogers-Ramachandran D. Sensations referred to a patient's phantom arm from another subjects intact arm: perceptual correlates of mirror neurons. Med Hypotheses 2008; 70: 1233–4.

Ramachandran VS, Rogers-Ramachandran D, Stewart M. Perceptual correlates of massive cortical reorganization. Science 1992; 258: 1159–60.

Rizzolatti G, Craighero L (2004) The mirror-neuron system. Annu Rev Neurosci 27: 169–192.

Rizzolatti G, Fogassi L, Gallese V (2001) Neurophysiological mechanisms underlying the understanding and imitation of action. Nature Rev Neurosci 2:661–670.

Rock I, Victor J. Vision and touch: an experimentally created conflict between the two senses. Science 1964; 143: 594–6.

Rose´n B, Lundborg G. Training with a mirror in rehabilitation of the hand. Scand J Plast Reconstr Surg Hand Surg 2005; 39: 104–8.

Roberts, TA; Smalley, J; Ahrendt, D (December 2020). "Effect of gender affirming hormones on athletic performance in transwomen and transmen: implications for sporting organisations and legislators". British Journal of Sports Medicine. 55 (11): 577–583

Royet JP, Plailly J, Delon-Martin C, Kareken DA, Segebarth C (2003) fMRI of emotional responses to odors: influence of hedonic valence and judgment, handedness, and gender. Neuroimage 20: 713–728.

Rozin R Haidt J and McCauley CR (2000) Disgust. In: Lewis M, Haviland-Jones JM (eds) Handbook of Emotion. 2nd Edition. Guilford Press, New York, pp 637–653.

Saxe R, Carey S, Kanwisher N (2004) Understanding other minds: linking developmental psychology and functional neuroimaging. Annu Rev Psychol 55: 87–124.

S. J. Russell and P. Norvig, Artificial intelligence: a modern approach (3rd edition): Prentice Hall, 2009.

Singer T, Seymour B, O'Doherty J, Kaube H, Dolan RJ, Frith CD (2004) Empathy for pain involves the affective but not the sensory components of pain. Science 303: 1157–1162.

Smith A (1759) The theory of moral sentiments (ed. 1976). Clarendon Press, Oxford.

Schilling, Vincent. 2017, indian country today

Stein, Stephen K. 2017, The Sea in World History: Exploration, Travel, and Trade

Simonsen R (2015) Eating for the future: veganism and the challenge of in vitro meat. In: Stapleton P, Byers A (Hg). Biopolitics and utopia. Palgrave Macmillan, New York (2015), S 167–190

Tesla N. "My Inventions", 1919

T. R. Society, "Machine learning: the power and promise of computers that learn by example," ed. The Royal Society, 2017.

Tomasello M, Call J (1997) Primate cognition. Oxford University Press, Oxford.